THE SECOND BOOK OF SOPRANO SOLOS

PART II

compiled by Joan Frey Boytim

G. SCHIRMER, Inc.

DISTRIBUTED BY

HAL•LEONARD®
CORPORATION
7777 W. BLUEMOUND RD. P.O. BOX 13819 MILWAUKEE, WI 53213

PREFACE

Many teachers have expressed the desire to have a second volume to complement *The Second Book of Solos* series for those high school and college students studying more advanced student literature. In my studio, I have found that students using the four volumes of *Easy Songs for Beginning Singers* in seventh and eighth grades move very easily into *The First Book of Solos* and *The First Book of Solos—Part II* in ninth and tenth grades. Several of my students have moved into *The Second Book of Solos* as early as eleventh grade. They would find the variety of *The Second Book of Solos—Part II* a welcome addition to their repertoire for eleventh and twelfth grades. With many of today's college freshmen using *The First Book of Solos* and *The First Book of Solos—Part II*, *The Second Book of Solos* and this new *Part II* will prove to be a great launching pad of further new repertoire for freshman and sophomores.

The songs introduced in this volume are on comparable levels of sophistication and musical difficulty with those found in *The Second Book of Solos*, and could be used at the same time to provide more variety of repertoire. Each voice volume has representative English, American, Russian, Italian, German, French, sacred, oratorio, and Gilbert and Sullivan selections not used previously in any of my other anthologies. There are a number of out-of-print songs which deserved to be reissued, and quite a number of unfamiliar songs which should find a place in student repertoire.

In these volumes we have been able to include pieces from more contemporary composers such as Barber, Bax, Bowles, Chanler, Duke, Dougherty, Hoiby, Ives, Griffes, Gurney, Lekberg, Sacco, Thomson, and Warlock. The relatively unknown French composer, Félix Fourdrain, is represented in three of the four volumes. These songs, as well as other unfamiliar French mélodies, have only been available in single sheet form and have never before had English singing translations. For these songs, a life-long vocal accompanist and retired French professor, Harry Goldby, has made very singable texts which relate very closely to the original poems. My excitement mounts when I think of those students who will enjoy learning many of these more unfamiliar songs, as well as those songs that have been difficult to find.

This set of four books will conclude the more advanced portion of this 16 volume basic series of teaching material for soprano, mezzo-soprano/alto, tenor, and baritone/bass (the four volumes of *The First Book of Solos*, the four volumes of *The First Book of Solos—Part II*, the four volumes of *The Second Book of Solos*, and now the four volumes of *The Second Book of Solos—Part II*). There are 528 different songs included in the 16 volumes, with an average of 132 songs of all varieties carefully chosen for content and suitability for each voice part. I only wish I had had all of these books for teaching when my studio began over 45 years ago!

Joan Frey Boytim
May, 2004

CONTENTS

ALLELUJA
from *Exsultate, Jubilate*

Wolfgang Amadeus Mozart
(1756-1791)

al - le - lu - ja, al - le - lu - ja, al - le - lu - ja, al - le - lu - ja, al - le - lu - ja, al - le - lu - ja, al - le - lu - ja,

* The accidental is a variant which appears in some editions.

al - le - lu - ja.

Al - le - lu - ja, al - le - lu - ja,

al - le - lu - ja, al - le - lu - ja, _____

al - le - lu -

8

* The lower note is a variant which appears in some editions.

9

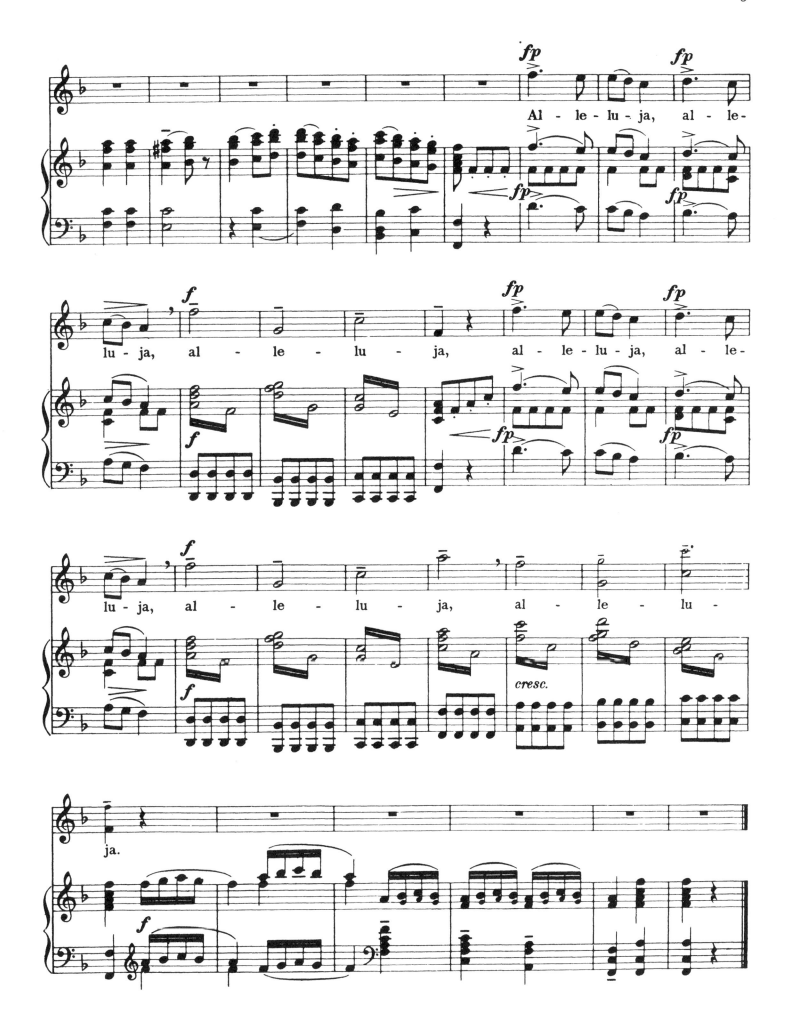

ALS LUISE DIE BRIEFE IHRES UNGETREUEN

(Louise Burns Her Love Letters)

Gabriele von Baumberg
English version by Lorraine Noel Finley

Wolfgang Amadeus Mozart
(1756-1791)

Ihr dan - ket Flam - men eu - er
You owe ex - ist - ence to a

Sein: ich geb' euch nun den Flam - men
fire, So to a fire I now re -

wie - der, und all die schwär - me - ri - schen
turn you; And you, his ar - dent songs, I

Lie - der, denn_ ach!— er sang nicht mir al -
burn you, For_ I was not his sole de -

lein. Ihr bren - net nun, und
sire. Be lost in flames! No

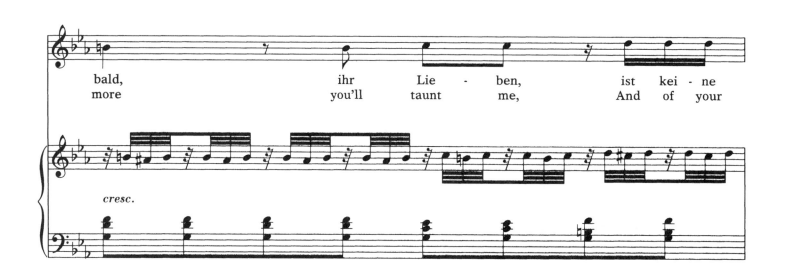

bald, ihr Lie - ben, ist kei - ne
more you'll taunt me, And of your

Spur — von euch mehr hier:
fond - ness euch leave no trace!

Doch ach! der Mann, der euch ge - schrie - ben, brennt
But oh! my lov - er's face may haunt me, And

lan - ge noch viel - leicht in mir, brennt lan - ge
burn my heart and fill your place, May burn for -

noch viel - leicht in mir.
ev - er in your place.

APRÈS UN RÊVE
(After a Dream)

Romain Bussine
English version by Theodore Baker

Gabriel Fauré
(1845-1924)

Dans un som - meil que charmait ton i - ma - ge,
Dreaming, to thee_ my_ heart I sur - ren - der;

Je rêvais le bon - heur, ar-dent mi - ra - - ge,
When I wake, where-fore dost thou ev - er van - - ish?

Tes yeux é-taient plus doux,_ ta voix pure et so - no - re, Tu ray - on -
How ra-diant were thine eyes,_ thy voice how ten - der! Fair thou as

nais com - me un ciel ___ é-clai - ré par l'au - ro - re.
skies whence the sun - shine night doth ban - ish.

son - - - - - ges,   Je t'ap-pel - le,ô   nuit, ___ rends-moi tes men-
tice ___ - - - me,   Should I a - gain ___ in thy love re-

son - - - - ges,   Re - viens,   re - viens   ra - di-
joice ___ - - me!   Be   mine,   be   mine   for ___

eu - - se,   Re - viens,   ô   nuit   mys - té - ri -
ev - - er,   Re - turn,   oh   love,   un - to   thy

eu - - - - - - se!
lov - - - - - - er!

LA BELLE AU BOIS DORMANT
(Sleeping Beauty)

André Alexandre
English version by Harry Goldby

Félix Fourdrain
(1880-1923)

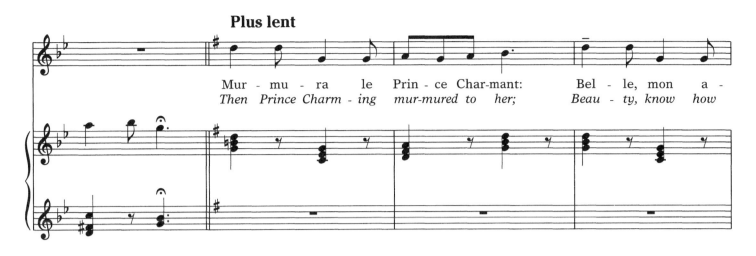

Plus lent

Mur - mu - ra le Prin - ce Char-mant: Bel - le, mon a -
Then Prince Charm - ing mur-mured to her; Beau - ty, know how

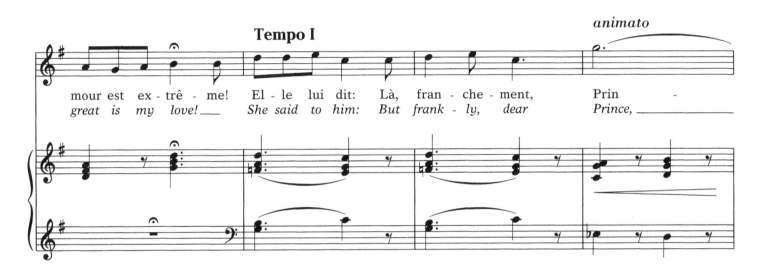

Tempo I *animato*

mour est ex - trê - me! El - le lui dit: Là, fran - che - ment, Prin -
great is my love!__ She said to him: But frank - ly, dear Prince,_____

rall. *a tempo*

- ce, il est u - sé vo - tre thè - me.
__ you're out of date with a line like that.

20

Moins vite

Veuil - lez donc pour cent ans en - cor
Go a - way for one hun - dred years
Re - tour - ner dans vo - tre pro - vin - ce;
Back to cast - les where you be - long;

retenez   *rit.*

Je rê - vais d'oi - seaux, de fleurs d'or
I was dream - ing of gol - den flow'rs
Et vous me dé - ran - gez, cher prin - ce!
And you've bro - ken the spell, dear prince!

Tempo I (scherzando)

Ain - si la bel - le s'ex - pli - qua
And so dear beau - ty pled her case
De - vant u - ne cour stu - pé - fai - te,
Look - ing at her stup - i - fied court,

Moins vite en cédant

opt.

Et tous lui re - pro - chaient dé - jà
They all re - proached her quite up - set:
Ce grave ou - bli de l'é - ti - quet - te,
This griev - ous breach of e - ti - quette,

21

to Bidú Sayão

THE BIRD

Elinor Wylie*

John Duke
(1899-1984)

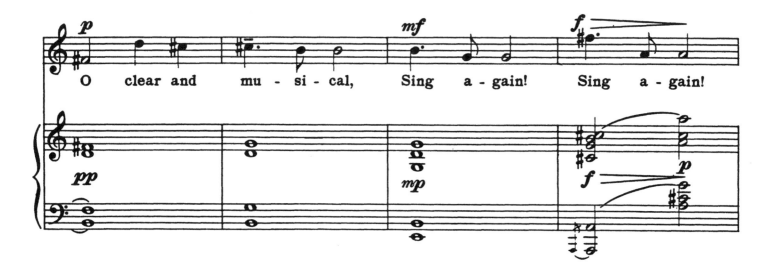

*Reprinted from "The Collected Poems of Elinor Wylie" by permission of Alfred A. Knopf, Inc. Copyright, 1932, by Alfred A. Knopf, Inc.

CARE SELVE
(Lovely woodland)
from *Atalanta*

English version by Shibley Boyes

George Frideric Handel
(1685-1759)

CHANSON NORVÉGIENNE
(A Norwegian Song)

André Alexandre
English version by Harry Goldby

Félix Fourdrain
(1880-1923)

Allegro moderato ♩ = 108

Je suis pri - se d'u - ne tris - tes - se
O - ver - come with dis - tress and sad - ness

Qui pè - se, pè - se lour - de - ment:
Which heav - i - ly weighs on my heart;

Il me tra - hit, il me dé - lais - se,
He be - trays me, he leaves me hope - less,

Ce - lui que j'ai - me ten - dre - ment.
He whom I love so ten - der - ly.

C'est fête au vil - lage et je dan - se,
It's the vil - lage fair and I'm danc - ing,

Pour ca - cher ma dou - leur, _____
To con - ceal my great pain, _____

hé - las!   Mais il me   sem - ble, á cha - que pas,   En -
A - las!   *But how it   seems, at ev - 'ry step,*   *I*

ten - dre cri - er   ma souf - fran   -   ce!
hear   all the cries   of   my   suf - fer - ing!

Au - des - sus_____ des fiords de Nor -
Far a - bove_____ the fiords of___

lar - mes, Et la dan - se n'ar - rê - te
plead - *ing,* *While* *the* *danc* - *ing* *stops* *not* *at*

pas,
all.

Mais il me sem - ble, à cha-que pas, Tour - no - yer_____
To me it seems,___ *at ev - 'ry step,* *I am swirl* -

rall.

dans   un   flot ____ de
in   the   flood   of   my

ing

a tempo

lar - mes!
tears! ____

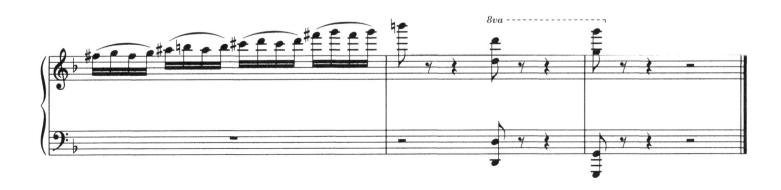

CLAVELITOS
(Carnations)

Joaquín Valverde
(1846-1910)

English version by Mrs. M. T. E. Sandwith

sen - cia, pre - sen - cia y po - ten - cia que usté ve - ra en mi!
die, For her heart was mine own And her love mine a - lone!

ten.

Cla - ve -
White car -

colla voce

a tempo

li - tos _____
na - tions! _____

a tempo

ten.   3

Que los trai - go bo - ni - tos _____ pa mi
Fair and pure as my true __ love! _____ Red car -

colla voce

DOMINE DEUS
from *Gloria*

Antonio Vivaldi
(1678-1743)

Largo

44

CRABBED AGE AND YOUTH

William Shakespeare

C. Hubert H. Parry
(1848-1918)

THE FIELDS ARE FULL

Edward Shanks

C. Armstrong Gibbs
(1889-1960)

Lento, dolcissimo ed espressivo

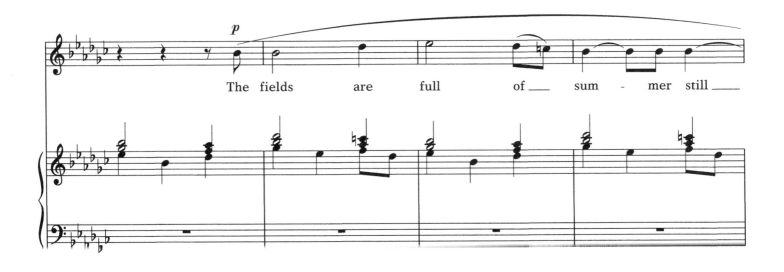

The fields are full of sum - mer still

And breathe a - gain up - on the air From

largamente

and ov - er full, _____ And

loved with _ strength, _ and loved with truth,

come primo

In heav - y

age are beau - ti - ful. _____

calando

Ped.

J'AI PLEURÉ EN RÊVE

(I wept, beloved, as I dreamed)

Gérard de Nerval
(after the German of Heinrich Heine)
English version by Carl Engel

Georges Hüe
(1858-1948)

J'ai pleu-ré en rê - ve;
I wept, be-lov - ed,

J'ai rê - vé que tu é-tais mor - te; Je m'é-veil-lai,___
as I dreamed thou hadst gone to heav'n-ly spheres; And when I woke___

___ et les lar - mes cou - lè-rent de mes jou - - es.
___ there burst from mine eyes a burn-ing flood of tears.

54

I MOURN AS A DOVE

from *St. Peter*

Julius Benedict
(1804-1885)

IL MIO BEN QUANDO VERRÀ

(When, my love, wilt thou return)

English version by Theodore Baker

Giovanni Paisiello
(1741-1816)

Il mi - o ben quan - do ver - rà
When, my love, wilt thou re - turn,

a _____ ve - der la ___ me - sta a - mi - ca?
Her _____ to see for ___ thee who is sigh - ing?

vien?   e'   il ____ mio ben,   ahi-mè!   non ____
me!   Ne'er I _____ see   re-turn!   Woe's ____

vien?____   e il mio ben ____   ahi-mè!   non _____ vien?
me! ____   ne'er____ I   see ____   re-turn!   Woe's _____ me!

Men   -   tre al-l'au - re   spie   -   ghe - rà
While   his   sweet-heart   on _____ the   air

la _____ 6 _____ sua fiamma,   i   suo - i   la - men - ti,
Wastes _____ her sor-row   in__ pi - ti - ful __ cry - ing,

mi - ti   au - ge - i   v'in - se - gne - rà   più
Re - spon - - sive moun-tains   her__ plaint   will__ bear,   More

dol - ci, più dol - ci ac - cen - ti.
gen - tly, more gen - tly re - ply - ing.

Ma non l'o - do.
Who can hear him?

E chi l'u - dì?
No voice hear I!

Ah! il mio be - ne am - mu - to - lì.
Ah! still my lov - er makes no re - ply.

Ah! am - mu - to - lì.
Ah! makes no re - ply.

64

THE LORD'S NAME IS PRAISED
(Praise the Lord ye servants)

Maurice Greene
(1696-1755)

70

The Lord is high a-bove all hea-then,

the Lord is high a-bove all hea-then,

and his glo - ry a-bove the heav'ns,

and his glo - ry a-bove the heav'ns, ____

heav'ns, _____ his glo - -

ry a-bove the heav'ns, a-bove the heav'ns, a-bove the heav'ns.

LOVE IS A PLAINTIVE SONG

from *Patience*

W.S. Gilbert

Arthur Sullivan
(1842-1900)

pure, _____ That is the love _ that's true! _____ Love that no
pure, _____ That is the love _ that's true! _____ Love that will

wrong can cure, Love that is al - ways new,⎫
aye en-dure, Though the re-wards be few,⎭ That is the love _ that's

pure, That _____ is ___ the love, _____ the love ___ that's

true! _____

MANDOLINE

Paul Verlaine
English version by Marion Farquhar

Gabriel Fauré
(1845-1924)

Les don-neurs____ de sé - ré - na - - des
Gal - lants fond - - ly ser - e - nad - - ing

Et les bel - - les é - cou-teu - - ses E -
And their la - - dies all__ at ease,____ Ex -

chan-gent des pro-pos fa - des, Sous les_ ra-mu - - res chan-ing
change ro-man - tic pat - ter, Be - neath the sing - - - ing

teu - - - - ses._____
trees. _____

C'est Tir - cis _____ et c'est_ A - min - - - te,
Here, Tir - cis* _____ and here,_ A - min - - - te,†

Et c'est l'é - ter - nel Cli - tan - dre,_____ Et c'est Da -
And e - ter - nal Cli - tan - dra,_____ And there, Da -

*Tir-cees
†A-man-ta

78

*Da-mees

MAUSFALLEN-SPRÜCHLEIN
(The Mouser's Magic Verses)

Eduard Mörike

Hugo Wolf
(1860-1903)

verhallend

schein, Mon - den - schein! _____ Mach' a - ber die
bright, *moon- light night!* _____ *Close win- dow and*

Tür fein hin - ter dir zu, hörst du? hörst du?
door; on en- t'ring, my dear, *d'you hear?* *d'you hear?*

Da - bei hü - te dein Schwänz-chen! hörst du? hörst du? Dein
lest your tail get a nip - ping! *d'you hear?* *d'you hear?* *A*

Schwänz-chen!
nip - ping.

MONDNACHT
(Moonlight)

Joseph von Eichendorff
English version by Arthur Westbrook

Robert Schumann
(1810-1856)

Teneramente, misterioso *(Zart, heimlich)*

schim - mer / von ihm nur träu - men
flow - ers, / *Might dream of re - gions*

müsst'. _____
blest. _____

Die Luft ging
The breeze stray'd

durch _____ die Fel - der; / die Aeh - ren
o'er _____ the mead - ows, / *And stirr'd the*

MY SWEETHEART AND I

Félix Bovet

Amy Beach
(1867-1944)

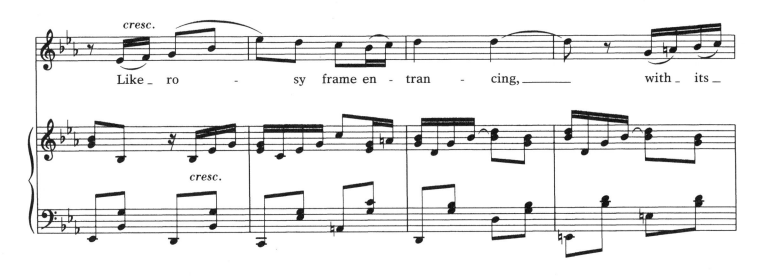

LE ROSSIGNOL DES LILAS
(The Nightingale and the Lilacs)

Léopold Dauphin
English version by Harry Goldby

Reynaldo Hahn
(1875-1947)

96

NIEMAND HAT'S GESEH'N
(No One Saw at All)

Otto Friedrich Gruppe

Johann Karl Gottfried Loewe
(1796-1869)

Ich
I

komm'__ in den Saal__ ge - gan - gen,__ da__ wim - melt's von Gä - sten
en - ter the hall,__ o - ver - flow - ing__ With__ com - pa - ny high and

bunt, wohl glüh - ten__ mir__ die__ Wan - gen,__ wohl__
low; Ah, how__ my__ cheeks__ were__ glow - ing,__ My__

glüh - te__ mir der Mund. Ich meint', es sä - he mir's je - der an, was
lips__ were__ all a - glow! Me thought: They'll see it, when I go in, How

Ich musst' hin-aus_ in den
Soon in - to the gar - den I

Gar - ten,_ und_ woll - te die Blu - men seh'n, ich
wan - der'd,_ To_ gaze_ on the flow'rs a - side; For

konnt' es_ nicht er - war - ten_ in den Gar - ten hin-aus zu
I_ could_ wait_ no long - er_ In the gar - den a-lone to

geh'n. Da blüh - ten die_ Ro - sen_ ü - ber-
*bide. There ros - es_ were bloom - ing on ev - 'ry_*

NON TI FIDAR

(Don't be too sure!)

from *Muzio Scevola*

English version by Shibley Boyes

George Frideric Handel
(1685-1759)

Non ti fi -
Don't be too

dar, per - chè il de - si - re lu - sin - ga è ver!
sure! Al - though de - sire's al - lur - ing, it's true,

mà poi so - ven - te A - mor è fal - so, fal - so,
rap - ture of __ love is of - ten fleet - ing, fleet - ing.

106

QUEL RUSCELLETTO
(The Brooklet)

Pietro Domenico Paradies
(1707-1791)

SORRY HER LOT WHO LOVES TOO WELL

from *HMS Pinafore*

W.S. Gilbert

Arthur Sullivan
(1842-1900)

eyes _____ that speak too plain - ly. Sor - ry her lot _____ who

loves _ too well, Heav-y the heart that hopes but vain - ly.

rall.

Un poco animato

Heav - y the sor - row that bows _____ the head When love is a -

cresc.

live _____ and hope _____ is dead! When love is a - live and

f

dim.

colla voce

hope _____ is dead!

Andante

Sad is the hour _____ when sets the sun— Dark is the

night _____ to earth's poor daugh - ters, When _____ to the ark _ the

wea - ried one Flies from the emp - ty waste of wa - ters.

Sad is the hour _____ when sets _ the sun— Dark is the night to earth's poor

Un poco animato

rall.

daugh - ters. Heav - y the sor - row that bows _____ the

p

cresc.

head When love is a - live _____ and hope ___ is dead! When

f

cresc.

f

dim.

p

love _____ is a - live and hope _____ is dead!

colla voce

p

f

SPRING

Thomas Nashe

Ivor Gurney
(1890-1937)

And we hear aye birds tune this mer - ry lay— Cuc - koo, jug - jug, pu - we, to - wit - ta - woo!

cresc.

ff

p

The fields breathe sweet, the

molto dim.

p

dai - sies kiss our feet, _____ Young lov - ers meet, _____

mf

allargando

a tempo

mf

f

Young lov - ers meet, old wives a - sun - ning sit _____

3

marcato

mf

Ped.   *

122

to Sara

SURE ON THIS SHINING NIGHT

James Agee*

Samuel Barber
(1910-1981)

*From "Permit Me Voyage". Used by permission of Yale University Press, Publishers.

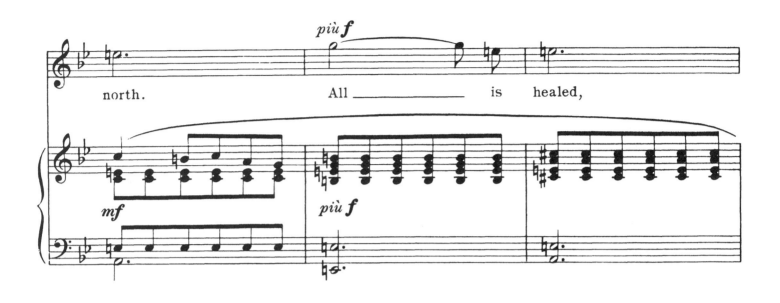

north. All _____ is healed,

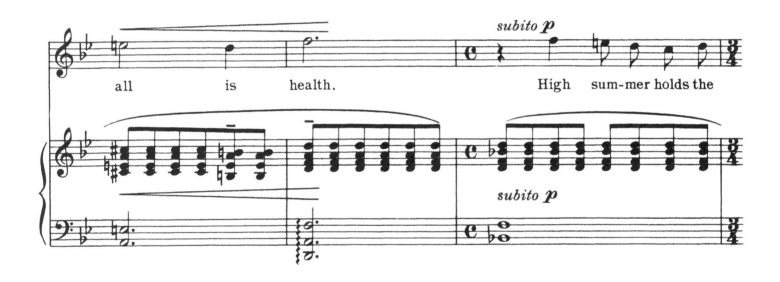

all is health. High sum-mer holds the

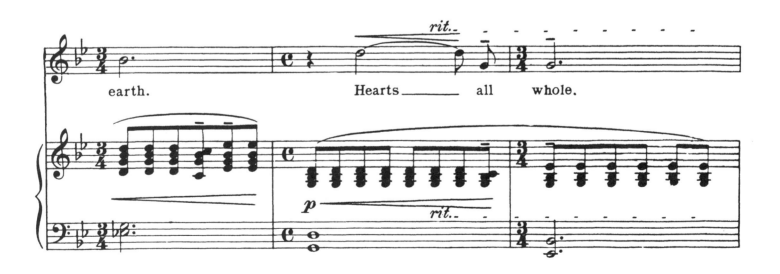

earth. Hearts _____ all whole.

STÄNDCHEN
(Serenade)

Franz Kugler
English version by Florence Easton

Johannes Brahms
(1833-1897)

Der Mond steht ü - ber dem Ber - ge, so recht für ver -
The moon hangs o - ver the hill - top, just right for young

lieb - te Leut'; _____ im Gar - ten rie - selt ein
folks in love; _____ The foun - tain mur-murs in the

Brun - nen, sonst Stil - le weit_____ und
gar - den, there's si - lence far_____ and

pp

breit.
wide.

Ne - ben der Mau - er im
Close to the wall in the

p

Schat - ten da steh'n der Stu - den - ten drei, mit
shad - ow three stu - dents are stand - ing by. With

Flöt'___ und Geig' und Zi - ther, und sin - gen und spie - len da -
vi - o-lin and flute___ and zith - er, They're sing - ing and play - ing the

bei,___ sin - gen und spie - len da -
while,___ sing - ing and play - ing the

bei.
while.

Die Klän - ge schlei-chen der
The sounds steal through to the

THAT'S LIFE

Josephine Royle*

John P. Sacco

*Words used by permission.

Once I hoped that For-tune would be kind But she nev-er smiled on me —

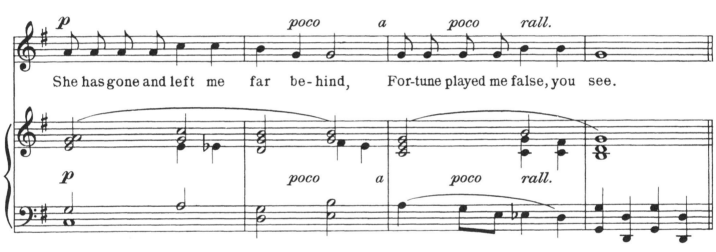

She has gone and left me far be-hind, For-tune played me false, you see.

Slower ♩=72

Ev-'ry-thing that I do Al-ways seems to fall through— Why it is I can-not ex-

plain! —___ And tho' the breaks sure are tough, Still I put up a bluff — That's

life, and it's so use-less to com - plain! I had learned to love you,

You said you were all through — I was driv - en al-most in -

sane, ___ For I had found, in dis-may, E-ven love can be-tray— That's

Faster ♩=116

life and it's so use-less to com-plain! Please tell me what life is all a-

bout, ___ I can't find out. Please tell me what love is all a-

WIND

Leonard Feeney

Theodore Chanler
(1902-1961)

Words used by exclusive permission.

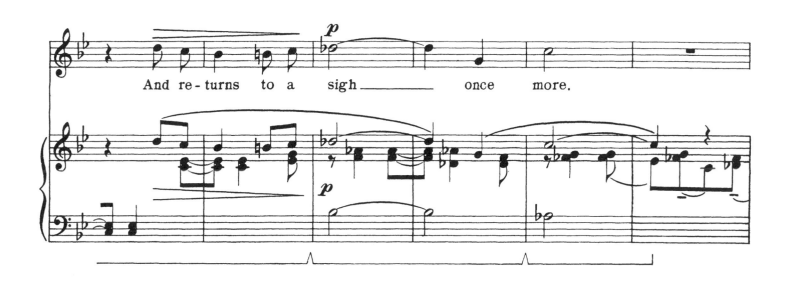

And re-turns to a sigh_____ once more.

Wind is the air In your hair,_____ When you stand On the sand By the

shore._____ Wind_____ will

shake the lat-tic - es late at night, It will

make the clouds go by; An - y - thing eas - y that's

hard to do, It is pret-ty sure____ to try:

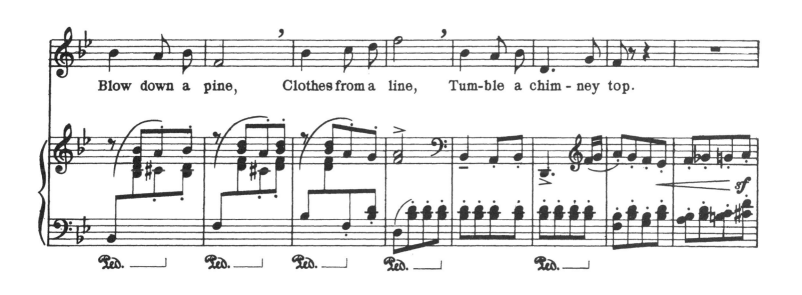

Blow down a pine, Clothes from a line, Tum-ble a chim-ney top.

Wind__ is the gen-er-al sound You hear a-round, That

sud-den-ly likes to stop.

Lento

THINK ON THESE THINGS

Adapted from
Philippians 4:4-8

June Caldwell Kirlin
(b. 1910)

true and love - ly, think on these things. If there

be an - y vir - tue, if there be an - y praise, re -

joice, re - joice in the Lord.

Think _ on these _ things, think on these things. Be

care - ful for noth - ing; but in pray'r and sup - pli - ca - tion let your re -

quests be known to God. _____ And peace will al-ways be with

you, _____ the peace of God be with you.

What - so-ev - er things are

TO ONE WHO PASSED WHISTLING THROUGH THE NIGHT

Margery Agrell

C. Armstrong Gibbs
(1889-1960)

Some - thing hath called me, Called me from far dreams. _____ The nak - ed

trees are quiv - er - ing with de - light.

Do dreams still __ hold me, That faint mu - sic

streams A-cross the haunt - ed si - lence __ of the

night?

Won - der hath ris - en,

Ris - en through the air. The

lis - ten - ing world in wor - ship

love - lier grows. Beau - ty hath

ris - en O how clear ___ and

THE WHITE PEACE

Fiona Macleod

Arnold Bax
(1883-1953)

ABOUT THE ENHANCED CDs

In addition to piano accompaniments playable on both your CD player and computer, these enhanced CDs also include tempo adjustment and transposition software for computer use only. This software, known as Amazing Slow Downer, was originally created for use in pop music to allow singers and players the freedom to independently adjust both tempo and pitch elements. Because we believe there may be valuable uses for these features in other musical genres, we have included this software as a tool for both the teacher and student. For quick and easy installation instructions of this software, please see below.

In recording a piano accompaniment we necessarily must choose one tempo. Our choice of tempo, phrasing and dynamics is carefully considered. But by the nature of recording, it is only one option. Similar to our choice of tempo, much thought has gone into our choice of key for each song.

However, we encourage you to explore your own interpretive ideas, which may differ from our recordings. This new software feature allows you to adjust the tempo up and down without affecting the pitch. Likewise, Amazing Slow Downer allows you to shift pitch up and down without affecting the tempo. We recommend that these new tempo and pitch adjustment features be used with care and insight.

The audio quality may be somewhat compromised when played through the Amazing Slow Downer. This compromise in quality will not be a factor in playing the CD audio track on a normal CD player or through another audio computer program.

INSTALLATION INSTRUCTIONS:

For Macintosh OS 8, 9 and X:
- Load the CD-ROM into your CD-ROM Drive on your computer.
- Each computer is set up a little differently. Your computer may automatically open the audio CD portion of this enhanced CD and begin to play it.
- To access the CD-ROM features, double-click on the data portion of the CD-ROM (which will have the Hal Leonard icon in red and be named as the book).
- Double-click on the "Amazing OS 8 (9 or X)" folder.
- Double-click "Amazing Slow Downer"/"Amazing X PA" to run the software from the CD-ROM, or copy this file to your hard disk and run it from there.
- Follow the instructions on-screen to get started. The Amazing Slow Downer should display tempo, pitch and mix bars. Click to select your track and adjust pitch or tempo by sliding the appropriate bar to the left or to the right.

For Windows:
- Load the CD-ROM into your CD-ROM Drive on your computer.
- Each computer is set up a little differently. Your computer may automatically open the audio CD portion of this enhanced CD and begin to play it.
- To access the CD-ROM features, click on My Computer then right click on the Drive that you placed the CD in. Click Open. You should then see a folder named "Amazing Slow Downer". Click to open the "Amazing Slow Downer" folder.
- Double-click "setup.exe" to install the software from the CD-ROM to your hard disk. Follow the on-screen instructions to complete installation.
- Go to "Start," "Programs" and find the "Amazing Slow Downer" folder. Go to that folder and select the "Amazing Slow Downer" software.
- Follow the instructions on-screen to get started. The Amazing Slow Downer should display tempo, pitch and mix bars. Click to select your track and adjust pitch or tempo by sliding the appropriate bar to the left or to the right.
- Note: On Windows NT, 2000, XP and Vista, the user should be logged in as the "Administrator" to guarantee access to the CD-ROM drive. Please see the help file for further information.

MINIMUM SYSTEM REQUIREMENTS:

For Macintosh:
Power Macintosh; Mac OS 8.5 or higher; 4 MB Application RAM; 8x Multi-Session CD-ROM drive

For Windows:
Pentium, Celeron or equivalent processor; Windows 95, 98, ME, NT, 2000, XP, Vista; 4 MB Application RAM; 8x Multi-Session CD-ROM drive